RUGBY UNION

Gill Lloyd
and
David Jefferis

Wayland

SPORTS SKILLS

Titles in this series:

Cricket Netball
Gymnastics Rugby Union
Hockey Soccer
Judo Tennis

Note In this book, the emphasis is on the full adult game. Mini-rugby (see page 28) has rules which introduce the game in stages, taking into account the physical and mental development of a child. These rules can be found in the *Rugby Football Union Handbook* and in a special booklet, called *The Rugby Continuum - Rules of Play*.

Photographs by Action Plus
Illustrations by James Robins and Drawing Attention
Consultant Des Diamond, Divisional Technical Administrator, Rugby Football Union

First published in 1993 by
Wayland (Publishers) Ltd
61 Western Road, Hove
East Sussex BN3 1JD, England

© Copyright 1993 Wayland (Publishers) Limited

British Library Cataloguing in Publication Data
Lloyd, Gill
  Rugby Union - (Sports Skills Series)
  I. Title II. Jefferis, David
  III. Robins, James IV. Series
  796.333

ISBN 0-7502-0700-0

DTP by The Design Shop
Printed and bound in Italy by Canale & C.S.p.A., Turin

Contents

Introduction

Rugby is a team game, played by fifteen people per side. They play together in a fast-moving contest for the ball. The aim is to score points by carrying the ball over the opposition's goal line and touching the ground with it, or by kicking it over the crossbar of the goalposts. The side which has the ball is more likely to score, so the game centres on the struggle to capture and keep the ball.

In rugby, you are allowed to handle the ball, run with it, pass it from one to another, kick it, or tackle an opponent who has possession of it.

▽ In most cases tries are scored through the work of several players. Supporting well and keeping an attacking movement going may result in a spectacular try such as this one scored by Japan in the Rugby World Cup in 1991.

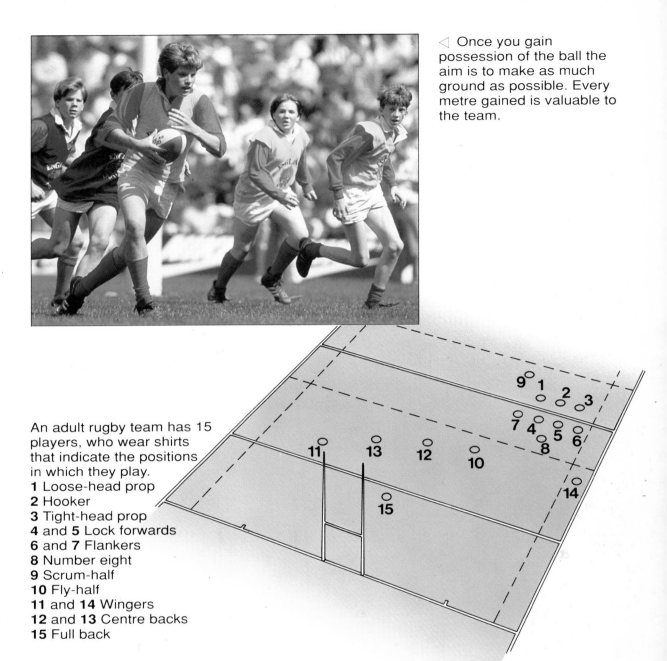

◁ Once you gain possession of the ball the aim is to make as much ground as possible. Every metre gained is valuable to the team.

An adult rugby team has 15 players, who wear shirts that indicate the positions in which they play.
1 Loose-head prop
2 Hooker
3 Tight-head prop
4 and **5** Lock forwards
6 and **7** Flankers
8 Number eight
9 Scrum-half
10 Fly-half
11 and **14** Wingers
12 and **13** Centre backs
15 Full back

Once you have possession of the ball, the object is to get it across the other team's goal line, or make ground with it. However, you are not allowed to pass the ball forwards. It is this rule that calls for all the players to work together - passing and running at speed towards the goal line. At its best, rugby results in thrilling sweeping movements up the field of play. A line of fast-running players swerve and side-step, passing the ball accurately from one to another, somehow finding gaps in the opposition defences, to score a try.

Getting started

If you go to a school that plays rugby, you are lucky. If not, there are many rugby union clubs that have junior sections. They usually play or train on Sunday mornings, providing coaching and games for boys and girls from six years of age upwards.

Rugby is played in shirts, shorts and long socks. All players on the same team wear identical clothing. Low-cut football boots with studs are usually preferred to the heavier boots with ankle protection. Shin guards, made of lightweight plastic, may be worn underneath your socks. Once you play rugby seriously, a properly fitted gum shield will help protect your mouth.

▽ There are some very exciting types of rugby for younger players. These games have simpler rules. The players can then work on their rugby skills - leaving it till later to learn about all the rules of the full game.

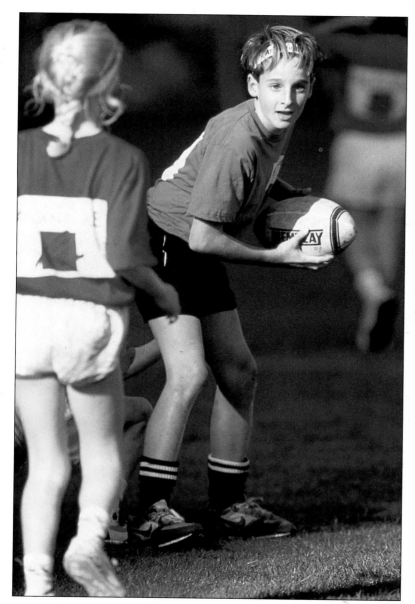

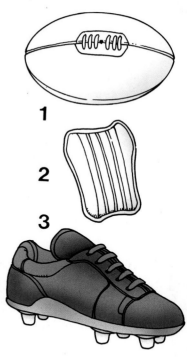

△ The basic equipment is very simple.
1 The ball is oval and there are three sizes. The smallest, size 3, is used for 6 to 9 year-olds, size 4 is for 10 to 14 year-olds. After that a full-size ball is used.
2 Shin guard.
3 Rugby boot.

◁ Boys and girls can practise their rugby skills together.

Fitness in rugby means having suppleness, strength, stamina and speed. If you are supple and flexible you will be less likely to end up with strains and sprains. Some simple warm-up stretches before a game or practice session will keep you supple.

Strength is a quality rugby players need to develop when they grow older. Stamina means having plenty of energy to keep going for a whole game. Running is one of the best ways to develop stamina. However, one of the greatest assets a rugby player can possess is speed. The ability to take off in an explosive sprint when you have the ball can make you a real star.

Rules and refereeing

There are four ways of scoring points in a rugby game. A try, worth five points, is scored by grounding the ball on or behind the opposing team's goal line. A successful try is followed by a kick at goal, a conversion, which is worth two more points. A dropped goal is scored during play when the ball is dropped from the hands on to the ground and kicked over the crossbar for three points. A penalty goal, worth three points, is scored from a place-kick awarded after a foul tackle or offside.

△ When a try is scored, the ball must be in the player's hands or arms as it makes contact with the ground. If the player falls on the ball, the front of the body - anywhere from neck to waist - must make contact with the ball.

Referees are in charge of play, but may take advice in senior games from touch judges. These use flags to indicate when the ball, or when a player carrying the ball, crosses the touch line.

▷ Rugby is played on a rectangular field, bounded by a touch-line along each side (**1**) and a goal line at each end (**2**). The goal posts are H-shaped and positioned on the goal lines. The area at each end of the field is called the in-goal area (**3**). There is a half-way line (**4**) and two 22-metre lines (**5**) marked on the pitch .

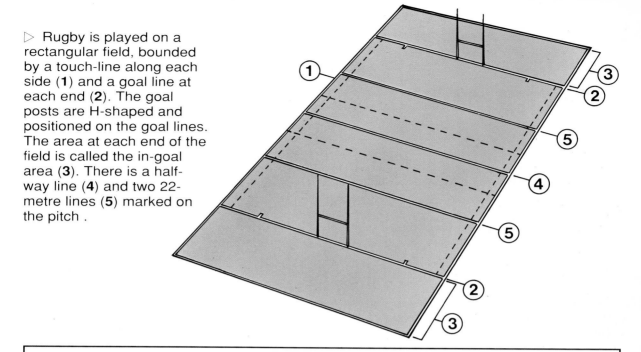

Referee's signals

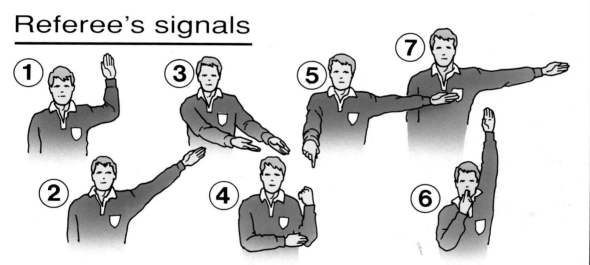

1 Free kick. Given to a player who makes a fair catch (a mark). Can also be awarded to the other side after minor offences. Goals cannot be scored directly from free kicks.
2 Penalty kick. Can be awarded to the non-offending side after a foul, such as an offside offence or a foul tackle. Generally,

players who are ahead of a team member with the ball are offside, and must not take part in the move.
3 Throw-forward. This is an offence. The ball must always be passed sideways or backwards.
4 Knock-on. Occurs if the ball goes forward after striking a player's hand or arm. Free kicks are

awarded for deliberate throw-forwards and knock-ons.
5 Scrummage or scrum. Restarts play after a foul, such as an unintentional knock-on or forward pass.
6 Successful try.
7 Advantage. Lets play continue if a broken rule has given an advantage to the non-offending team.

Handling the ball

Despite its oval shape, the rugby ball is easy to catch. But if it hits the ground, it is difficult to know which way it will bounce. So the skills of gathering a ball are not as easy to learn as holding, passing and catching. Learn to pick up the ball at speed, in one continuous movement. Run alongside the ball, keeping your eyes fixed on it. Bend down and scoop one hand underneath it, the other in front, to stop the ball being knocked-on.

Sometimes it is too difficult to pick up a loose ball and you may have to fall on it to stop the other team getting possession. Use your body as a screen for the ball, by falling on to it with your back to the opposition. Once you have done this, you have to get up with the ball immediately or release it on the ground.

◁ Bending down and picking up a loose ball is not a simple task with the ball bouncing in odd ways. You need to keep calm and keep your eye on the ball.

Passing

When passing the ball, hold it in front of you (**1**) and look up to identify the player to whom you are passing (**2**). Throw the ball just in front of your team-mate, aiming at chest height (**3**). The receiver should be able to run into the ball, rather than having to stop and take it.

◁ When you are in possession of the ball, try to hold it with both hands, one each side of the middle. If you clutch the ball between your hands and body, you will not be able to move it quickly in response to a challenge, or get enough movement to carry out a pass. Here, England player Jeremy Guscott is perfectly balanced to make a pass. He is aiming carefully at his team-mate.

Running with the ball

Seeing a player with the ball weaving past defender after defender is a thrilling sight. The main tactics for getting by defenders are the side-step, swerve, hand-off and dummy pass.

The swerve can get you past a defender on the outside of the pitch. Run towards the defender, aiming slightly in, towards the centre of the field. This will check his or her speed, and keep space in the outer field. With the defender moving towards the centre, swerve back towards the outfield and accelerate away.

Changes of pace while you run can deceive defenders, but one of the best actions is the dummy pass. For this, you go through the motions of a real pass up to the moment of releasing the ball. The defenders follow what they assume to be the ball's path, while you escape upfield, still in possession of it!

△ Tucking the ball under an arm enables you to run faster. It leaves the other arm free to hand-off, fending away an opposing player with your open hand.

△ Jonathan Webb of England takes on the Australians, his weight on his outside foot, in preparation for a sudden side-step.

▷ The side-step is the tactic of wrong-footing a defender by a sudden change of direction.
1 In order to outwit your opponent, it is necessary to run with real commitment, disguising your intentions until your opponent is close.
2 Choose your moment to stamp your outside foot down hard, using it to push off in the opposite direction.

Kicking

◁ A powerful and well-balanced follow-through is an important part of a kick. See how New Zealand player Grant Fox still has his head down and his eyes on the ball.

Kicking is an important rugby skill. An accurate kick at goal is a good way to gain points. Kicks out of defence can be used to get your team out of trouble and to take play away from your own goal line. A kick into touch in defence can give your side a little breathing space. In attack, the advantages of putting the ball behind the opposing defence has to be weighed against the possibility that you may lose possession.

Dribbling a rugby ball, moving it along the ground close to your feet and under control, is not easy, but it can be a very useful technique to use if the ball is wet and slippery and hard to pick up.

Place-kick

A place-kick is used when attempting a kick at goal from a penalty or after a successful try, and to start a match after an interval. The ball is placed on the ground and kicked from there. Aim to hit the ball with the top of your kicking foot, which should make contact just below the centre of the ball. Point your foot down from the ankle and make a good follow-through to finish the kick.

Drop-kick

A drop-kick is used to score a goal during play or to score from a penalty. You drop the ball in front of you, pointed end down, and kick the ball as it bounces. It must touch the ground for a dropped goal.

Punt

The punt is the kick used most during the course of a game. It can be a distance kick, a short but high 'chip', or a short kick along the ground, known as a grubber. Drop the ball and kick it straight from your hands before it bounces.

Tackling

A player with the ball may be held and brought to the ground. The aim of a tackle is to stop your opponent and regain possession of the ball. Holding opponents is important - it is not enough to just knock them over or trip them up. If the player you have tackled is off his or her feet and held, it is a fair tackle and the ball must be released. Tackling a player without the ball, and tackles around the head and neck, are forbidden.

The first point of contact in a tackle should be your shoulder, followed immediately by a tight wrapping action of your arms around your opponent's legs. You can tackle from the side, front-on or from behind.

Side tackle

The side-on tackle is the most common one to use. Drive in low and make shoulder contact with your opponent's thigh, keeping your head behind his or her buttocks. Wrap your arms around the thighs and pull tight. Hold on and land on top of your opponent.

Front tackle

For the front or head-on tackle, arrive at a slight angle. Drive in low, with your shoulder aiming at the line of the shorts and thigh, keeping your head to one side of your opponent. Wrap your arms around the thighs and hold on tight. Twist to land on top of your opponent.

◁ A smother tackle is one that aims to stop your opponent making a pass with the ball, by covering the ball with your arms or body, as you make your tackle.

▽ The tackle from behind is the most difficult to make. Having made contact, the tackler hangs on to the opponent, acting as a dead weight. You might slide down the legs to accelerate the fall.

Tackle from behind

Tackling from behind is similar to other types. Keep your head to the side and away from your opponent's legs.

Forward play

The major role of the forwards is to win the ball. They need to work together as a unit, to get possession in scrums, line-outs, rucks and mauls. In the scrum the forwards bind together and push against the opposing team, head-to-head. The ball is put in between the front rows of the scrum, and the hooker tries to hook it back through the legs of the other forwards. It can then be passed from the rear of the scrum by the scrum-half.

Line-outs are a very important source of possession. If the ball goes out of play over the touch-line, the two sets of forwards line up at right angles to the touch-line and parallel with each other. The ball is thrown in straight between the two lines of players.

△ The forwards at work in a ruck. Rucks and mauls occur during the course of play. A ruck is a form of loose scrum when the ball is on the ground and opposing players push for possession. A maul is formed by one or more players from both sides around the ball carrier.

▷ The forwards are usually referred to as 'the pack'. The loose-head prop (**1**) and the tight-head prop (**3**) are the heftiest players in the side and have to support the hooker (**2**), the middle player in the front row who hooks the ball back with his foot. The lock forwards (**4**, **5**) form the second row of the scrum. They are usually the tallest and heaviest players in the team and have the added job of jumping, to win the ball at line-outs. The flankers (**6**, **7**) help hold the scrum together, but are well positioned, so that they can break away as soon as the ball leaves the scrum. Known simply as number eight (**8**), this player gives power and control at the back of the scrum.

▽ The front five are the power house of the team.

Power of the scrum

The most effective means of gaining the advantage in a scrum is by pushing the opposing side backwards. This is why a strong and heavy pack is useful. Good tight binding of the players on to each other makes for a solid scrum.

Simply by squeezing arms and gripping hard, the scrum can exert great pressure. Good body position is also important, not only for power but for safety. Heads should be raised, stomachs and hips pushed towards the ground and backs straight. Feet should be splayed and knees bent, to help get the maximum forward shove.

△ Looking down the tunnel between the two sides. In order to get possession, the ball has to be hooked from the tunnel to the back of the scrum. It can then be safely collected and fed to the backs. In mini-rugby, the emphasis should be only to restart the game. Real power is not so important until a player is adult.

The scrum-half of the non-offending team puts the ball into the scrum. He or she must stand one metre away, midway between the opposing front rows, hold the ball in both hands between the knee and ankle, and put the ball in without delay and with no dummy actions. There is an advantage if your side has the put-in. Your team's hooker is slightly nearer the ball than the hooker of the other side.

Offsides

At scrums, rucks and mauls, a player is offside if he or she is in front of the offside line. This is an imaginary line that runs parallel with the goal lines and through the back foot of the rear player in the scrum, ruck or maul.

Adjusting the scrum

Your side must bind together tightly before you engage with the opposition scrum. You then drive into them in one step, keeping your feet firmly in position. A pack has to learn to lock against, or counter a push from the opposition.

The line-out

In a scrum, you have an advantage if your side is putting the ball in. In a line-out however, each side has a reasonable chance of gaining possession. You can win the ball in a variety of ways. The ball can be caught and held by a good jumper. It can be passed or deflected by a jumper, out to the scrum-half, or to another player in the line-out.

Whatever line-out tactics are used, a good throw-in is a vital first step. The ball needs to be delivered at the right speed and height or all the efforts of the line-out will be wasted. The one-handed spin, or torpedo throw, is the most popular method to use.

▷ In this line-out example, the throw is taken by the team that did not play the ball before it went into touch. This team decides the number of players (usually seven) in the line-out. The two lines of players stand one metre apart. All other players, except for the opposing hooker and the two scrum-halves, must be behind the off-side line (**1**), an imaginary line drawn 10 m either side of the line of touch (**2**).

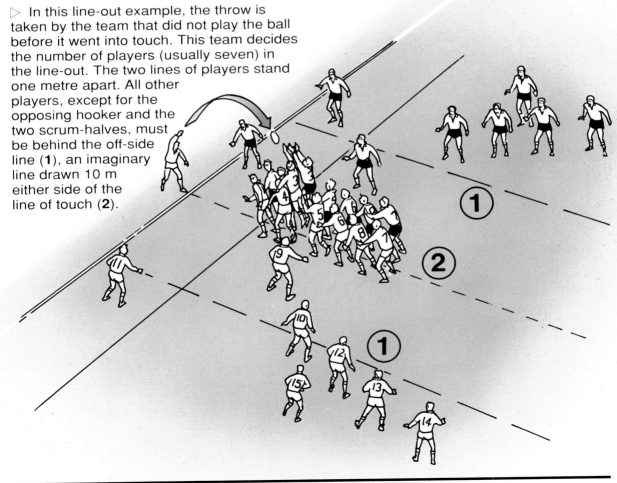

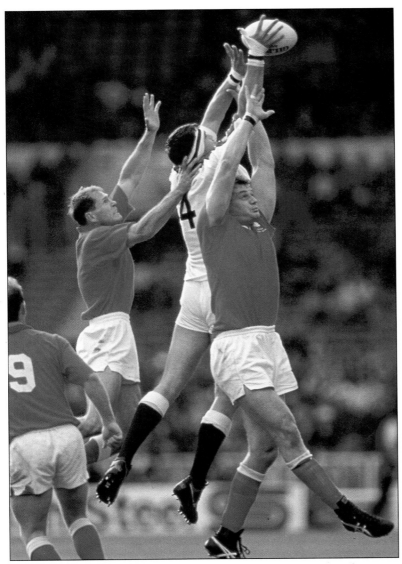

Palming the ball (using the inside arm only) from the line-out is not just a case of jumping and hitting the ball. You need to be thinking about directing the ball to your scrum-half or to a team-mate. Here, England player Martin Bayfield out-jumps two Canadians.

Catching with two hands is difficult in a line-out, because of the interference from other players. However, if someone does make a brilliant two-handed catch, the other forwards have to help get the ball out to the scrum-half. The wedge movement is one way of doing this. The players on either side of the 'jumper' bind firmly on to the jumper and drive forward. The jumper catches the ball and turns in the air to face the scrum-half, presenting his or her back to the opposition.

△ To throw in, hold the ball towards one end, with your fingers. Raise the ball above your head, then, leading with the elbow of the raised arm, use your wrist and fingers to propel the ball towards the target.

Half-back play

The scrum-half is the link player between the forwards and the backs, guiding and directing their efforts and making decisions once they have the ball. Because it is a linking position, the scrum-half must have a complete range of skills.

You must be able to pick up the ball quickly and pass it, be able to kick, feed the scrum accurately and tackle well. A good scrum-half also has to be able to pass the ball off the ground straight to the backs. If you are under pressure, the dive pass is an effective technique.

△ A dive pass is made when you approach the ball from behind, directly in line with the receiver. Get your feet close to the ball, sweep it up cleanly and throw it with a dive.

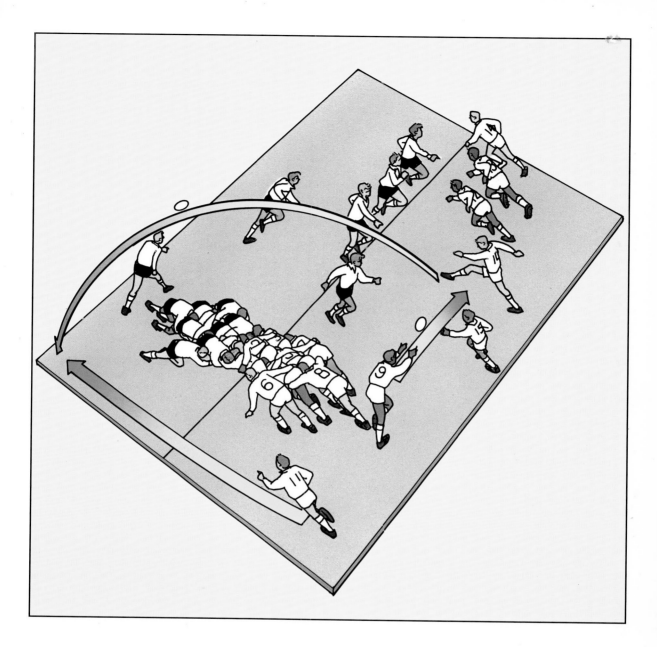

The fly-half or outside-half must be able to read a situation quickly and decide what to do with the ball. Would it be best to start a passing movement, or should the ball be kicked upfield?

If you are the fly-half, you must be able to catch everything that comes to you and transfer the ball with accurate passes to the centres. You are responsible mainly for the team's tactical kicking.

△ The high kick ahead and the long diagonal kick are mainly used for gaining ground. It is important that the team should follow the kick rapidly, to try to win back the ball as quickly as possible.

The three-quarters

The three-quarters are the left and right wingers and the two centre backs. To play these positions you need the skills of swift, sure handling and strong tackling. You have to do a lot of running, both in attack and defence, and be aware of the positions of your team-mates so that you can make quick decisions if unexpected situations occur. Your particular handling skills should include a good range of passing movements, along with running skills such as the swerve, side-step, change of pace and dummy pass.

△ Here, the black defence has driven the white attack across the field. The ball is now with the wing three-quarter, usually one of the fastest members of the team, who needs to sprint very quickly to get to the line and score a try.

The gain line (**1**) is an imaginary line drawn across the field at the point where initial possession is gained. Here, it passes through the centre of a scrum. Teams are always trying to get a ball carrier beyond the gain line.

You need to be able to kick to touch from defence, as well as make short chip and grubber kicks in mid-field. Making hard tackles at speed and being able to win the ball are also crucial. However, your best attack weapon is speed. To be a good three-quarter you need to develop sprinting ability. You must be able to accelerate rapidly over a short distance.

The full back is the last line of defence, so has a big responsibility. You must be a capable and confident tackler, because when the full back has to make a tackle it is often a vital one. Another full back function in defence is to catch and gather kicks, particularly high balls.

The ability to kick far and accurately is necessary. You may have to kick the ball into touch, with the opposing team chasing after you, and no one to back you up if you make a mistake. Because kicking skill is such an important part of being a full back, you are usually called upon to take the place-kicks.

Good opportunities for attack may come from situations when the opposition is kicking the ball towards you or the wings. The full back may get the chance to start some counter-attacking moves.

◁ When catching high balls there is always a risk of collision with other players, possibly your own wingers. Give a loud call to let everyone know you are going for the ball. Keep your eyes on the ball, and make a cradle for it with your arms, clutching it close to your body as you make the catch.

Rugby for young players

Mini-rugby has been developed as a game for younger players. It gives them a good and safe grounding in the skills of rugby. The numbers in a team vary, from five at six years old, to twelve at eleven years old. The full game is introduced gradually in a series of stages, until the early teens, when the full, adult game, can be played.

Mini-rugby is played on a pitch of appropriate size. For example, players who are under twelve years old use a pitch that measures about 50 x 60 metres.

▽ The rules for mini-rugby are similar to the full game, except that no fly-kicking (an uncontrolled kick at the ball) is allowed. Conversions are taken under the cross-bar for players under ten years old. Under-eights do not kick conversions at all.

New Image is a running-and-passing game of touch rugby, in which the ball must be passed as soon as the player with it is touched correctly. Teams are made up of forwards and backs. Any number can play, but with no more than five forwards, as the game is mainly about running and passing.

In New Image, line-outs are not contested. The ball is caught above head height by a member of the team throwing in. The scrum must hold firm with no pushing allowed. The opposition cannot strike for the ball.

△ Only tries can be scored in New Image rugby and players are not brought down when tackled. The tackler must touch the player with the ball with two hands, one on either side of the hips. The tackled player has to pass the ball immediately to a team-mate. No forward passes are allowed.

Glossary

Advantage law
The referee can allow play to continue after an infringement (such as a foul) if stopping play would be a disadvantage for the non-offending team.

Conversion
A successful kick over the cross-bar to convert a try into a goal. Worth two points.

Dribbling
Kicking the ball along the ground under full control.

Drop-kick
The ball is dropped from the player's hands and kicked as it rebounds from the ground.

Fair catch
A catch inside your own 22-metre line, made with one foot on the ground. For a fair catch, you must catch the ball directly from a kick by an opponent, shouting 'mark' as you make it.

Free kick
Awarded to a player making a fair catch, or to a member of the non-offending side after an infringement. A goal cannot be scored directly from a free kick.

Kick-off
This starts the game in the form of a place-kick from the centre of the half-way line.

Knock-on
The act of knocking the ball forward, towards the opposing goal line, with hands or arms, the ball then touching either the ground or another player.

Line-out
The method by which play is re-started after the ball has been carried, knocked or kicked out over the touchlines. Teams form parallel lines, and a player from the team which did *not* touch the ball last throws in.

Maul
Formed by the ball carrier and at least one player from each side, in contact around the ball.

Offside
If you are ahead of a team member who is in possession of, or has kicked the ball, you are offside.

Penalty goal
A goal scored from a penalty kick. Worth three points.

Penalty kick
Kick given to a non-offending side for a breach of the rules. Such breaches may include foul tackles or offside offences.

Place-kick
A kick made after placing the ball on the ground. This is the usual kick for converting a try.

Punt
Kicking a dropped ball before it hits the ground.

Ruck
Formed when players from both sides gather over a grounded ball.

Scrum
The means of restarting play after a rule infringement. At least five forward players, (and usually eight) join together in a binding formation that then interlocks with the other team. The ball is put in between the legs of the two front rows. This space is known as the tunnel.

Tackle
Grabbing the player with the ball so that he or she is brought down to the ground.

Throw-forward
A forward pass, illegal in rugby.

Touch
The ball goes into touch when it contacts or passes over the touch-lines at the sides of the playing field.

Try
A try is scored when a player grounds the ball correctly on or over the opposing team's goal line. It is worth five points.

Books to read

Rugby Union: The Skills of the Game, Barrie Corless (The Crowood Press, 1985)
Rugby Union (Play the Game series), Ian Morrison (Ward Lock Limited, 1989)
Take Up Rugby Union, John Shepherd (Springfield Books Limited, 1989)

For teachers and coaches:
Even Better Rugby, Rugby Football Union (The Crowood Press, 1992)

Index